# *ideals*®

## HOMESPUN

In the calm of a cool shady valley
    At the edge of a rippling rill,
There's a cottage so restful and rustic
    Nestled close in the arms of a hill.

There's repose in that quaint little cottage
    Away from all hurry and strife.
There I feel the fruits of my striving
    Are not the true values of life.

There's a stillness, a beautiful stillness,
    Away from the city's mad din,
Where God and his comforting presence
    Have a chance to come quietly in.

As I sit in the soft fading twilight
    Lovely harmony enters my heart.
The music of God has a chance to be heard;
    All nature seems tuned to take part.

The rustle of wind in the oak trees,
    The song of the proud mockingbird,
The ripple and splash of the wandering brook
    Make a symphony joyfully heard.

There the cares of the world are forgotten
    And I'm free from all fears, stress, and strain.
There I gain a new strength and fresh courage,
    And quiet peace is mine once again.

Men boast of their riches and travels,
    Their prestige and possessions, but still,
I'll not trade that quaint little cottage
    Nestled close in the arms of a hill.

Mazie Halliday Binnion

**Editorial Director,** James Kuse

**Managing Editor,** Ralph Luedtke

**Associate Editor,** Colleen Callahan Gonring

**Production Editor/Manager,** Richard Lawson

**Photographic Editor,** Gerald Koser

**Copy Editor,** Sharon Style

# Lovely July

Oh, beautiful, wonderful month of July
With green growing fields and clouds sailing high,
The long golden days—every shining new dawn,
And dewdrops that sparkle on morning's bright lawn.

Oh, shimmering fields in the wonder of day,
The warmth of the sun blessing summer's bright way,
The gardens of God where the roses are fair
And fragrance is rich on the soft gentle air.

Dear, lovely July, when hearts hold a dream,
When shadows are tall and a peace reigns supreme.
The beauty of nature as birds sing their song,
Each dear country road—stretching out wide and long.

The leaves sigh and murmur—the brook ambles on,
The dusk whispers softly as daylight is gone,
Fireflies flit in gladness, in evening's warm sky
And hearts hold so fondly to lovely July.

Garnett Ann Schultz

ISBN 0-89542-325-1  295

IDEALS—Vol. 36 No. 5 July MCMLXXIX, IDEALS (ISSN 0019-137X) is published eight times a year,
January, February, April, June, July, September, October, November
by IDEALS PUBLISHING CORPORATION, 11315 Watertown Plank Road, Milwaukee, Wis. 53226
Second class postage paid at Milwaukee, Wisconsin. Copyright © MCMLXXIX by IDEALS PUBLISHING CORPORATION.
All rights reserved. Title IDEALS registered U.S. Patent Office.
Published simultaneously in Canada.

ONE YEAR SUBSCRIPTION—eight consecutive issues as published—only $15.95
TWO YEAR SUBSCRIPTION—sixteen consecutive issues as published—only $27.95
SINGLE ISSUES—only $2.95

The flower garden has been a cherished part of household gardening in America during the past two centuries. Although grim necessity had to come first in the very first gardens of the New World, flowers for flowers' sake quickly followed. And when the westward trek began, flower seeds were squeezed into jammed storage quarters of the pioneer wagons, to spread their delicate beauty across the continent.

We have selected a handful of popular flowers to talk about—most of them still widely grown—and another handful of flower-growing activities. It is a kind of eavesdropping visit, a listening to voices of generations ago talking of their flower loves and fancies, yet shot through with surprisingly timely and practical advice.

MIGNONETTE takes its name from the French for "the little darling." It is normally an annual, but if given winter protection it will grow, said Old Peter Henderson, into a woody shrub known as tree mignonette and commonly thought of as a different species. If grown in too-rich soil, mignonette loses its fragrance—its most prized quality. To have mignonette in the house in winter, Henderson directed, sow seed in pots outdoors in July, thinning to no more than eight plants to the pot. About September bring the pots into a cool room to form flower buds. In October move them to the light in a room that "does not exceed 50° at night," where they will flower beautifully until March.

PANSIES have been among the favorite annuals of gardeners for many years, being as willing to grow as they are lovely. Here is how a Harrisburg, Pennsylvania gardener of the later 19th century handled her planting from one year to the next: "Year before last we sowed pansy seed about the first of May, in the ground, but put window glass a little raised over the spot and kept the ground always moist. They came up beautifully. When quite small we transplanted them six inches apart along the edge of a bed in a small shady backyard. From the first of August until the frosts came we had the finest pansies we ever saw outside a greenhouse. Late in the fall we prepared a very rough coldframe against the south side of the house, carefully lifted each plant and set them close together in this place. In February they began to bloom. Bouquets were cut every day, not one bloom was allowed to go to seed or wither on the stalk, and by this means they were kept in bloom until the first of May. The same stalks bloomed all summer in the open ground, having been cut back and set out in May. Self-sown seedlings almost as fine are now [the following spring] blooming in the coldframe."

ROSES. In 1876 *The American Agriculturist* had this advice on growing this perennial indoors in winter: "Be sure that the roses have been grown in pots, and not taken up from the open ground and potted, as they rarely recover in time to be of much use. As to soil, it matters little what it is, provided it is porous, as liquid manure may be used if it is poor, but if it becomes soggy and close, the plants will fail. Roses when growing need at most a temperature of 70° in the daytime, and it may go fifteen or twenty degrees lower at night. Do not overwater; always let the soil get a little dry on the surface before watering. Turn the ball of earth out of the pot occasionally, and see if there are angle worms; if they cannot all be picked off, water with clear lime water. Shower as often as convenient; once a week at least, but twice or three times is better; set

# Flowers For Today

the pots in the bathtub or sink, and shower with a fine sprinkler. If plant lice [aphids] appear, shower with weak tobacco water. Sudden changes of temperature and cold drafts are apt to cause mildew, and should be avoided in airing. When a shoot has bloomed, cut it back to a good bud; do not be afraid to use the knife."

For those interested, this advice was offered in 1878: "The budding of roses should be attended to during the months of August and September. The buds should be inserted upon the north side of branches that have completed their growth for the season. A fine effect is produced by budding different kinds of roses upon the same stalk."

TUSSIE-MUSSIES. That charming conceit, the tussie-mussie, is still as appreciated today as in colonial times. Its construction is precise, a central flower surrounded by smaller ones. For instance, a large rosebud is encircled with white alyssum, then there may be a circle of forget-me-nots, one of tiny pink rosebuds, another of lavender ageratum, and finally a circle of mignonette for fragrance. The stems of all are passed through an X-slit in a lace paper doily, a rubber band holds the doily around the stems and the stems are wrapped with foil.

We make tussies with whatever the garden offers at the time. Several hours beforehand we gather the flowers and put them in water at once; it is best to do so right in the garden as you gather them, then keep them in a cool dark place until ready for arranging. Have facial tissue or paper napkins, depending on the size of the tussie to be made, folded in three or four thicknesses and in widths suited to the length of the stems. Starting with the central flower held in the left hand, arrange the first circle around it and just slightly lower; then wrap tissue or napkin three or four times around the stems. Repeat this procedure with each of the other flower circles. Then surround the whole with rather stiff leaves such as those of Martha Washington geraniums or camellia. At this point, if the tussie is not to be presented immediately, we immerse the stems in a glass of water. When ready to complete the little thing we dry the stems with a towel, wrap another layer of paper around them, slip the doily on, and mold a piece of foil around the stems right up to the leaves and flowers. If you have hardened the flowers well, the arrangement will last for hours, even when carried in a warm hand—which is what a tussie-mussie is for.

We have made them from tiny four-inch-wide ones, on up to glamorous foot-wide kinds in a spectrum of color and form. For a festival queen and court we harmonized flower colors with gowns and added streamers of inch-wide ribbon with love knots holding tiny flowers represented in the bouquets. Two of the most appreciated ones were made of only Martha Washington geraniums because they were all that the garden had in perfection at the time. We selected two colors, one for each tussie, for two small girls who were assistant hostesses at their artist-grandmother's one-woman show.

For real fun, try a vegetable tussie. Start with a fine fresh and plump radish with its little tail root left on. Hold it upside down and surround it with curled parsley. Follow with a circle of tiny carrots, then with a circle of an herb—thyme, basil, or marjoram—and frame the whole with nasturtium leaves. There—a delicious, old-fashioned bouquet.

Ken and Pat Kraft

# The Intriguing Love

Jenny Kay

The most priceless of all
Gifts of love is the giving
Of oneself, understanding
Another's needs for growth
To find his self-understanding.

A person is like a bud
Whose numerous soft petals
Shield vast vibrant
Levels of consciousness.

Love, like the tender gardener,
Nurtures the bud to its
Fullest awareness,
Patiently awaiting the
Brilliance of the blossom.

The tool of this love of a person
Is the artist, who plants
His love in the soul of man,
And reaps, perhaps, nothing?

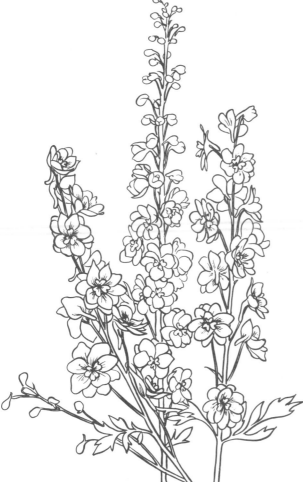

The beauty of a soul
lies in the flower of its production,
so that one may produce
a dandelion or a rose.

# Alice Leedy Mason

Alice Leedy Mason, a long-time favorite of Ideals readers, is as warm and sunny as the Blue Ridge Mountain summer morning on which she was born. Among her memories of growing up in Virginia are ventures up those mountains and gatherings at the horse stable in the town below, where Mrs. Mason would entertain her friends with poetic recitations, usually including "The Children's Hour." During the late 1950's, her own poetry became a special feature of "Bert Parks Bandstand" where "Just a Housewife" prompted a guest speaker of the program to suggest Mrs. Mason for "nomination for President." Today, she and her husband live in Milwaukee where Mrs. Mason, in addition to a full-time job, keeps busy knitting for her two grandchildren, writing children's mystery novels, and translating books into braille. This same concern and love for others which characterize Mrs. Mason's life is also reflected in her poetry; she expresses her ultimate goal with the words, "If it is my privilege to leave 'footprints' for others to follow, please let mine be words to the praise and glory of God."

## Boots

The streets are glistening in the rain;
The puddles quickly form
Beneath the feet of all who choose
To venture in the storm.

It might be wise to stay at home,
That seems the safer part.
But boots can skip across the ponds
When summer's in the heart.

## The Big Pretense

Whenever I grow tense with fear,
Alone with all my cares and ills,
I close my eyes to troubles here
And lift them up unto the hills.

I see the rhododendron grow
Beside each rock and rill.
A tree frog croaks, sweet violets show,
And rabbits scurry up my hill.

A gentle wind picks up my fear,
The scent of pine my faith refills,
For God must see me standing here
Pretending I can see the hills.

## Just a Housewife?

"I'm just a housewife," that's what she said!
And apologized with a toss of her head.
Just a housewife? I don't agree.
I'm glad this position was open for me.

Our duties are different as occasions arise.
Do I have your permission to open her eyes?
She's a housekeeper, homemaker, warm-hearted friend,
Dietitian, nurse with patients to tend.

She's a mediator, manager, booster, chef,
Critic and agent, both in a breath;
A chauffeur, listener, counselor, judge . . .
With a faith in her family that nothing can budge.

She's "the lady of the house" to the passerby,
A hearer of lessons, a "private eye."
She's a wealth of suggestions, someone who cares,
A kisser of bruises, a listener to prayers.

She's a master at making the little things do,
From last year's pajamas to leftover stew.
A homemaker? Yes! Just a housewife? Never!
To hold down this job you've got to be clever!

## Blue Ridge Morning

The hills are rounded, stretching tall
Above the fields of green.
Here a brook, an orchard there,
With ground fog in between.

Beyond the hills, the mountains stand.
Their shoulders touch the sky.
The sun leans down to clear the mist
And welcome passersby.

## This I Believe

This I believe, in spite of care,
If I a smile of friendship wear
And do, in truth, my hand extend,
I make the fiercest foe my friend.

If discontent has been my lot
And mere existence on the spot,
I'll find no place of greater worth
Though I should search the face of earth.

If I give just a crust of bread
To see God's creatures amply fed,
There comes into my meager cup
A banquet fare from which to sup.

I love a church whose open door
Bids welcome to both rich and poor.
This I believe—I never feel
So near to God as when I kneel.

## The Waiting World

There's many a fool
Will throw in the tool
When he thinks the job is too tough.
The man worthwhile
Is the one who can smile
Whenever the going gets rough.

There's many a plan
That's wrong for a man
Could he but see the return.
To be on his way
He must honestly say,
"I'm ready and willing to learn."

For life is a job
And trouble may rob
The heart of its reasons to try.
The door just ahead
Is the one that we dread,
But pass it and obstacles fly.

Now life is a cinch
If bought by the inch,
By the square yard, it's a chore.
The man who begins
And fights till he wins
Is the man that the world's waiting for.

# Harry S. Truman, The Homespun President

Truman, as described by Roy Roberts, the then managing editor of the Kansas City *Star*, as "The epitome of the 'average man'—a quality he felt might prove Truman's 'greatest asset,' for it would enable him to understand the people's needs."

Born in Lamar, Missouri, on May 8, 1884, Harry S. Truman learned early the value of hard, honest work. As a boy on his paternal grandparents' farm where his family lived, he had the same chores as any other American farm boy. Even when his family moved to Independence, Harry had chores to do and cattle to pasture before and after school. And he excelled in school, doing extra studies whenever he could in the hopes of securing an appointment to West Point or Annapolis. He was denied admittance, however, due to his poor eyesight. When his father's business failed, Harry went to work for the Santa Fe railroad, keeping track of the hours the migrant workers put in and then paying them at the end of the week. Along with the modest salary and board, he also received an excellent education on how to handle men. After the railroad job, Harry became a bank clerk, a job from which he was promoted so often that in five years his salary had gone from $35 a month to $125. When his maternal grandfather retired and Harry's father took over the farm, Harry was expected to come home and help manage things, which he did very well, putting the farm in the top brackets of American farming. His farming proved to be as much a challenge for him as his banking, and he did just as well. His profits from the farm were invested in oil drilling until a shortage of manpower developed, due to the start of World War 1.

Harry's military career began in the National Guard; and when he entered the Army, he was made a first lieutenant of the 129th Field Artillery of the 35th Infantry Division. Upon his arrival in France, he was promoted to Captain and placed in command of an artillery battery. The Army became a perfect school in dealing with the practicality of human relationships.

Upon Harry's return home, he married Bess Wallace, his childhood sweetheart and opened a haberdashery with an Army buddy. Unfortunately, the store was forced to close, due to the Depression, leaving both men heavily in debt.

Truman had been interested in politics since he was sixteen, when he went to the Democratic National Convention in Kansas City with his father. While in France, Truman served with Jim Pendergast, grandson of the Democratic party boss Tom Pendergast. Jim suggested Truman for the position of "county judge," whose duty was to levy taxes, maintain the county roads as well as build new ones, and maintain county institutions. Truman won the election, starting a long, often controversial political career as Senator, Vice-President, and finally after the death of Franklin D. Roosevelt, President. Truman loved people and had a history of voting for the worker, the common man.

Despite the controversy of Truman's Presidency, which often comes with the Office, Truman was greatly loved by the people. Even the newspapers who heavily criticized him during his Presidency, admitted after his retirement that through his hard work he had been a devoted public servant to the people.

Shari Style

# Family Day

It is from the family that a child first learns how to be a responsible citizen. In recognition of the part the family unit plays in strengthening the nation through its children, President Johnson proclaimed the first Family Day in 1968. This commemorative day was a result of the combined efforts of Kiwanis International and the Freedoms Foundation at Valley Forge.

Family Day 1979 will be observed Sunday, August 12. This year's theme has been declared "Family Responsibility—the Strength of Nations;" and festivities will emphasize the need for teaching basic moral truths and values to the nation's children. Observances across the country on this special day will include reunions, picnics, parades, and church services—all activities designed to savor that special closeness and love so vital to the family unit.

Today's family is, indeed, the cornerstone of tomorrow's society. By proclamation of the highest office in the land, we honor each family, large and small.

# Homespun Folks

Just homespun folks, the common kind,
A cleanliness of heart and mind,
Rough-woven like a homemade quilt,
Healthy, and strong, and sturdy-built
To weather every wind that blows,
A heartiness that warms and glows.

Just homespun folk with no pretense
Blessed with the gift of common sense,
The cheerful workers of the earth,
(How little do we prize their worth)
Dependable as oak and pine
To do their best in rain or shine.

Edna Jaques

# Grandparents' Day

We would like to thank our readers for their response to help establish a national Grandparents Day. An official proclamation for a national Grandparents Day was made by President Carter in 1978, and will be celebrated the first Sunday after Labor Day, this year, September 9, 1979. By the strengths and moral fiber set by our elders, and the love and steadfastness they have shown, we hope all grandparents will be recognized and appreciated for their contribution to our society.

# My Mother Read to Me

My mother read to me the tales
   Of pioneers of old,
Who forged ahead with strength and hope
   To worlds rich with gold.

She read to me the soothing poems
   That put the heart at rest,
The epic poems of gallant knights,
   Of bravery put to test.

While seated at my mother's knee
   And listening to her voice,
We journeyed merrily about
   To countries of our choice.

She read of Christ and what he taught
   To guide our every day.
She read of rich adventure
   In lands across the way.

I'm thankful that she read to me,
   For echoing through the years
Are joyful times we shared with books
   That linger bright and clear.

Craig E. Sathoff

 # Animal Crackers

Animal crackers, and cocoa to drink,
That is the finest of suppers I think;
When I'm grown up and can have what I please
I think I shall always insist upon these.

What do you choose when you're offered a treat?
When Mother says, "What would you like best to eat?"
Is it waffles and syrup, or cinnamon toast?
It's cocoa and animals that I love most!

 The kitchen's the cosiest place that I know:
The kettle is singing, the stove is aglow,
And there in the twilight, how jolly to see
The cocoa and animals waiting for me.

Daddy and Mother dine later in state,
With Mary to cook for them, Susan to wait;
But they don't have nearly as much fun as I
Who eat in the kitchen with Nurse standing by;

And Daddy once said, he would like to be me
Having cocoa and animals once more for tea!

Christopher Morley

From the book SONGS FOR A LITTLE HOUSE by Christopher
Morley. Copyright 1917, renewed 1945 by Christopher Morley.
Reprinted by permission of J. B. Lippincott Company.

Madelyn Stanchfield Trebilcock

# The Talking Machine

On a gentle August evening
As the summer sun burns low,
Creaking sounds come from the porch swing
Where you're talking with your beau.

You hear noisy crickets chirping
And the next door neighbors laugh,
While your favorite songs are playing
On the parlor phonograph.

Before the age of motion pictures, radio, television, and modern stereo systems, the Edison phonograph supplied a main source of entertainment. People who did not play a musical instrument or sing could still have music in their homes. With a turn of the crank, they spent hours listening to their favorite tunes, from "On the Mississippi" and "The Trail of the Lonesome Pine" to "Whistling Rufus One-Step" and "The Americans Come."

The idea for this ingenious "talking box" was formulated in the mind of the young inventor Thomas Alva Edison. Though partially deaf from the age of twelve, Edison had always been fascinated by the study of sound; and devices that repeated sound held a particular interest for him. Edison had become well acquainted with the theories of sound reproduction and, earlier, had invented a carbon transmitter that increased to two hundred words per minute the speed by which a telegraph message could be recorded and repeated. Stimulated by the inventions of the telegraph in 1844 and the telephone in 1876, he intended to apply the theories of sound reproduction to the telephone. Engrossed in a search for a method of recording and reproducing telephone conversations, he did not immediately foresee the result of his experimentation.

On July 18, 1877, however, Edison announced his intention to invent a phonograph. He had discovered the basic principle of the phonograph—a diaphragm that vibrated in tune with the voice. The vibrations of the diaphragm could be recorded by a small pin onto a surface.

Four months later, Edison gave his workman, John Kruesi, a sketch from which to work. The only advice he offered was, "The machine must talk." Kruesi proceeded to build a brass and iron contraption that consisted of a tinfoil-covered cylinder on a shaft turned by a hand crank, plus two diaphragms—one to speak into and one, hopefully, out of which to hear. No one, including Edison, expected successful results. The only hope was that the experiment would provide another key to the mechanical reproduction of sound.

The experiment not only provided a key, it provided the answer. When Kruesi had completed construction of the machine, Edison turned the crank and spoke into one of the diaphragms. The pin attached to it dug grooves into the surface of the cylinder. Replacing this diaphragm with a second one, he turned the crank again. To the listeners' astonishment, the phonograph repeated, very distinctly, Edison's high-pitched voice:

Mary had a little lamb,
Its fleece was white as snow,
And everywhere that Mary went
The lamb was sure to go.

Although the words were less than profound, they were significant as the first human sounds to be mechanically recorded and reproduced.

After patenting the phonograph, Edison continued to develop and improve it, extending its use on a broad scale. In an article published in a leading magazine, he outlined his ideas on the future of the phonograph; most of these ideas would someday be put into effect, such as its use in recording dictation, music, books for the blind, and lessons for educational purposes. For several years Edison's company produced talking dolls that recited nursery rhymes on tiny Edison phonographs. This same principle has been revived in recent years with the advent of dolls that talk with the pull of a string. A more important adaptation of the phonograph occurred when certain companies fitted it with a coin-slot mechanism. This machine served as the original jukebox. In later years, disks developed by Edison replaced the cylinders. Gradually the phonograph evolved into the stereos of today. Just as importantly, it served as the basis for future inventions, such as the tape recorder, radio, television, and other means of recording and reproducing sound yet to be invented.

Of the 1,033 devices Edison patented, the phonograph is among those that have had the most lasting and far-reaching effects. With this instrument he succeeded in capturing the human voice, music, and all sound for future generations.

Beverly Rae Wiersum

# Porches

There's something homey in a porch—
  The large old-fashioned kind
That's built across a home's front side
  To form a welcome sign.

The porch is not screened in or closed
  But open to the weather,
And open, too, for neighbors who
  Just like to get together.

If I could find the perfect porch,
  I'd like to have it be
A meeting place in summertime
  For cookies and iced tea.

A cat would doze upon its rail
  In graceful calm repose.
In pots that set upon its steps
  Geraniums would grow.

Some chairs would casually be placed
  For those who stay a bit—
A wicker rocker, big and deep,
  An oak bench next to it.

No porch could ever be complete
  Without the wooden swing,
That's such a restful way to spend
  The summer evenings.

There's something friendly in a porch—
  The large old-fashioned kind,
Where good deep-rooted friendliness
  You're always sure to find.

Craig E. Sathoff

# Sweet Music

The old-fashioned brass band has done more, to my way of thinking, than any other one thing to make our country the great nation that it is. The yeast of democracy never bubbles harder than when two dozen barbers and grocery clerks and farmers tear into "Dixie" or "Columbia, the Gem of the Ocean."

In my day a brass band marching down Main Street on a Fourth of July and bursting forth with "Yankee Doodle" was positively the grandest sight on earth. On it marched, with firecrackers popping all around. I remember once when a small boy tossed a cannon cracker into the bell of a bass horn. It made the loudest and most explosive note ever to come out of a horn.

The more runaways a band caused, the better it was liked. In my home town every Fourth of July parade caused an average of three runaways. When the band came abreast of a skittish team of geldings, they would rear up on their hind legs, and then amidst the screams of women and the cries of children the terrified horses would plunge down the street. I know of nothing that gave a person more downright wholesome excitement than a team of runaway horses.

Parents who exercised careful and profound judgment in assisting their sons in choosing a band instrument were well rewarded. If a boy had buck teeth and a receding chin, a wise father steered him away from a horn. Squint Peabody was a perfect case of matching the boy to his instrument. Squint had a mouth that puckered like a black sucker's, giving him a perfect downdraft for a piccolo.

Of course, a two-hundred-pound man looks a bit ridiculous as he clutches a piccolo against his bosom and waits through almost an entire musical selection until it comes his turn to blow a few tweets. He feels that life has sort of passed him by. But on the whole, piccolo players get as much fun out of life as anybody. In our band we always ranked the piccolo player as a pantywaist. We thought he blew a little more into a piccolo than he ever got out of it.

Picture in your mind's eye the town park on a balmy summer evening with the bandstand gaily lighted and with the gold braid and the gold buttons of the musicians' uniforms reflecting little beads of light. There comes a dramatic pause in the music—and then the cornetist rises and points his horn heavenward. With bated breath the audience follows the silvery notes until, finally, the band director's baton drops to his side. The cornetist resumes his seat amid a thunderous wave of applause.

Any man who can remember back to the time he played a silver cornet solo need never feel that his life has been lived in vain.

Not far behind the cornetist in prestige was the trombone player. You could spot a trombone player's wife any time because she was so thin and pale and nervous. Any woman who had to listen to her husband practicing a trombone smear night after night for weeks was bound to have bulging eyeballs and the whim-whams.

In the good old days a town was rated by the number of musicians in its band and by the elegance of their uniforms. A brass band with an oboe and a French horn was considered very deluxe.

Financing a band often was a serious problem. Some bands had to play in the red year after year. But loyal boosters of a really progressive town took it upon themselves to raise a band fund every year. It was understood this fund was to be used to buy uniforms; then, if there was a balance remaining, that, according to well-established precedent, was to go for an oyster supper.

Unfortunately, for some reason, band players were very fond of oysters. I remember our band boys once voted to treat themselves to oyster suppers very early in the season. Nobody seemed to keep in mind the exact amount of the surplus, and it turned out the boys ate so many oysters that the new uniforms, figuratively, went down their throats.

It's my firm conviction that when the small town band went out, treason, disloyalty, and subversive activities came in. I just can't imagine a subversive band member; he blew all his primitive urges right out through his horn. And it was hard for the bystander to feel anything but complete loyalty when the boys got wound up and ripped into Sousa's March. Rural life lost something fine and honest when our band played its last concert; we haven't been the same since.

R. J. McGinnis

# UNCLE SAM

Imaginary symbol of our land?
  Uncle Sam was a real man!
Tall, loose-jointed, genial gent
  Long typified our government.

Poor farm boy who bred success,
  Heroic mold of the new U.S.
Trusted, revered by the folks he knew,
  Epitome of an American true . . .

Yes, there was a real man behind our national symbol, Uncle Sam. The life story of "Uncle Sam" Wilson is one of a humble farm lad struggling for success, and reflects the struggle of a young America.

Born September 13, 1766, in Massachusetts, Sam Wilson spent his younger years helping to raise twelve brothers and sisters; and the post-Revolutionary depression left young Sam with no money. He moved westward with his brother in 1789, where they settled in Troy, New York. Here Sam combined honesty with good common sense and hard work to start several lines of small businesses. It was his meat-packing venture, however, which provided Sam his chance for fame.

The Wilson brothers became the chief suppliers of meat and munitions to American Army troops in the War of 1812. A chief customer, Army contractor Elbert Anderson, always marked his barrels E.A.U.S.—the last two letters, of course, standing for the United States. An amusing story developed that the U.S. was short for Uncle Sam Wilson, the man who was selling the Army its food. Soon the soldiers began to call all their supplies "Uncle Sam's." Even the federal government employees in Washington adopted the new term. When the war ended, trustworthy, reliable, country-devoted "Uncle Sam" had come to symbolize the national character of the government.

The drawings and cartoons we have seen probably don't resemble what Sam really looked like. He was, however, tall and slim, but he never wore a stars-and-stripes costume, nor did he ever have a beard. These features were added by cartoonists shortly after Uncle Sam became a national symbol.

In 1961, Congress adopted a resolution saluting Sam Wilson as the "progenitor of the American national symbol." Because of his friendliness and strict integrity, the citizens of Troy would have long remembered Uncle Sam Wilson, even if he had not been the forefather to inspire the national symbol we affectionately know as "Uncle Sam."

Linda Robinson

# Let Freedom Ring!

At noon on the Fourth of July every year, our independence is celebrated in the atmosphere of 1776 by a traditional commemorative ceremony aptly called "Let Freedom Ring." The place is Greenfield Village, a museum near Detroit, Michigan.

The festivities begin with a parade led by the museum's town criers in authentic costumes of the colonial period. The Greenfield Village Volunteer Militia and the Greenfield Village Players (all in the dress of the times) follow, with a horse-drawn open coach bearing the museum officials and speakers of the day bringing up the rear. The main event takes place on the steps of the museum's replica of Independence Hall.

People who gather to witness the pageant feel the impact of the proceedings, particularly as the ceremony moves to its climax. The town crier reads selections from the Declaration of Independence; the militia fire a volley from their muzzle-loading rifles; and the bell in the tower (an exact replica of the Liberty Bell) tolls the glad message of freedom and independence.

Greenfield Village, a comprehensive museum which presents to the visitor a full-scale panorama of American life as our forefathers knew it and lived it, is located on a 200-acre setting in Dearborn. It was conceived by Henry Ford, who said, "When we are through we shall have reproduced American life and preserved in actual working form at least a part of our history and our tradition." And a great part it is!

Greenfield Village is comprised of one hundred historic buildings that have been moved from various parts of the country and restored in meticulous detail. To name a few, there are the frontier courthouse in which Abraham Lincoln first practiced law in Logan County, Illinois; Thomas Edison's laboratory, moved from Menlo Park, New Jersey; the Wright Brothers Shop ("Birthplace of Aviation") moved from Dayton, Ohio, under the personal direction of Orville Wright; and the Clinton Inn, which was once a nineteenth century stage-coach stop between Detroit and Chicago.

Watching craftsmen plying their trades, common in the time of the birth of our nation, adds to the pleasure of one's visit. Twenty-two buildings house the tools and handiwork of pre-industrial workmen, such as the Gun and Locksmith Shop or the candle-making shop where antique molds are used in demonstrating that ancient art.

In the building devoted to the history of the locomotive, stand examples of engines dating from the tiny 1829 Rocket to a 600-ton Allegheny of 1941.

It couldn't be a Henry Ford Museum without an area devoted to restored antique automobiles—steam, electric, and gasoline-propelled.

On Independence Day one can—in his imagination—turn back the years and relive the excitement of that historic moment of almost two hundred years ago when a courageous company of men signed the document that gave them—and us—freedom and the right to pursue happiness in our own way!

Doris Paul

# The Georgia Goat Man

A grizzly beard, a twinkling eye,
  the preacher travels long;
His only roof the spacious sky,
  he joins the birds in song.

He travels light, his supper seeks
  among those who will give,
And on them blessings he bespeaks
  and prays their sins forgive.

The Lord is his companion true,
  no structure keeps Him in;
The preacher values freedom, too,
  and seeks peace from within.

In simple things he finds his joy,
  in tending to his flocks;
His cross and Bible are his ploy,
  good tidings he unlocks.

Oh travel-weary, travel-wise,
  you preacher of the road,
Take up your cross, lift up your eyes,
  and Peace you will behold.

Shari Style

Part of America's rich past is the travelling preacher. Often a very colorful, odd individual, the preacher made his way from town to town, literally preaching for his supper. One such "modern-day" preacher was Charles "Goat Man" McCartney, the nickname acquired from his vast herd of goats which he frequently drove down the highways, much to the dismay of motorists. Collecting money from passengers on a bus from Macon to Jeffersonville, Charley the Goat Man built a one-room church, which he later used as his home. Above the door hung a crude cross and his old wagon sat outside, reminiscent of past wanderings. Times do keep changing, but now and then a bit of the past creeps out to remind us of our ever mobile, colorful heritage.

David Quinn

# Beside the Stream

We wandered over the rolling land,
    Up little hills and down;
While overhead the roving clouds
    Were drifting toward the town.

We came upon a winding stream
    With water crystal clear,
And saw the golden grains of sand
    And pebbles shining here.

The cattails grouped along the banks
    And blue forget-me-nots;
While crayfish scuddled out of sight
    To hide in sheltered spots.

The dragonflies flew here and there
    And tadpoles moved about;
The minnows swam in gleaming schools
    And frogs jumped in and out.

We could hear some buzzing insects
    And chirpings in the trees,
While the balmy air was fragrant
    With hay to scent the breeze.

The water rippled on its way—
    A pleasant rhythmic sound;
And we were filled with happiness
    With this beauty all around.

Harriet Whipple

# A Child's Day

I wandered through a shady lane
   Among the birds and bees;
A pretty yellow butterfly
   Went dancing through the trees.
I chased him over broken boughs
   And grasses green and cool.
He settled just beyond my reach,
   Inside the lily pool.

So I sat down upon the grass
   To rest awhile, and doze.
He tasted of the lilies
   And he whispered to a rose.
I watched him flitting to and fro,
   Until I fell asleep,
But wakened when he softly came,
   And kissed me on the cheek.

I'm glad that God made butterflies,
   And taught the birds to sing.
His love and goodness all around
   I see in everything.
So I shall try to show my thanks
   By being loving too.
I'll wear a happy loving smile,
   And pass it on to you.

Agnes Wells

# The Companionship of a Child

A child's eyes,
those clear wells of undefiled thought,
what on earth can be more beautiful?

Full of hope, love, and curiosity,
they meet your own.
In prayer, how earnest;
in joy, how sparkling;
in sympathy, how tender!

The man who never tried
the companionship of a little child
has carelessly passed by
one of the great pleasures of life.

Mrs. Norton

# Ode to a Butterfly

Thou spark of life that wavest wings of gold,
Thou songless wanderer mid the songful birds,
With Nature's secrets in thy tints unrolled
Through gorgeous cipher, past the reach of words,
    Yet dear to every child
    In glad pursuit beguiled,
Living his unspoiled days mid flowers and flocks and herds!

Thou winged blossom, liberated thing,
What secret tie binds thee to other flowers,
Still held within the garden's fostering?
Will they too soar with the completed hours,
    Take flight, and be like thee
    Irrevocably free,
Hovering at will o'er their parental bowers?

Or is thy luster drawn from heavenly hues,—
A sumptuous drifting fragment of the sky,
Caught when the sunset its last glance imbues
With sudden splendor, and the tree-tops high
    Grasp that swift blazonry,
    Then lend those tints to thee,
On thee to float a few short hours, and die?

Birds have their nests; they rear their eager young,
And flit on errands all the livelong day;
Each fieldmouse keeps the homestead whence it sprung;
But thou art Nature's freeman,—free to stray
    Unfettered through the wood,
    Seeking thine airy food,
The sweetness spiced on every blossomed spray.

The garden one wide banquet spreads for thee,
O daintiest reveller of the joyous earth!
One drop of honey gives satiety;
A second draught would drug thee past all mirth.
    Thy feast no orgy shows;
    Thy calm eyes never close,
Thou soberest sprite to which the sun gives birth.

And yet the soul of man upon thy wings
Forever soars in aspiration; thou
His emblem of the new career that springs
When death's arrest bids all his spirit bow.
    He seeks his hope in thee
    Of immortality
Symbol of life, me with such faith endow!

Thomas Wentworth Higginson

# The Priceless Things

Give me a golden sunbeam
That dances through the trees,
One single note that songbirds
Let drift upon the breeze.

Capture for me some starlight
Or bits of falling rain,
The peace and real tranquility
That fills a country lane,

Caress me with a dewdrop
That holds a world of bliss,
And I will be contented
With Mother Nature's kiss.

A speck of blue from out the sky
Or Mr. Moon's warm glow,
And I will have the things I need
To conquer all my woe.

Embrace all this with tenderness
That comes when people smile,
And I will have the essence of
What makes this life worthwhile.

Ben Burroughs

# The Story of the Isle of Man: One Thousand Years of Parliamentary Rule

*In 1979 the Isle of Man, a nation of approximately 60,000 people, celebrates one thousand years of unbroken parliamentary government. Each year, the island strives for agricultural self-support. Although fishing is not the thriving industry it once was, scallops and Manx kipper still account for large exports. Situated almost equidistant from England, Scotland, Ireland, and Wales in the Irish Sea, however, Man's most important industry is tourism. One-half million people from the British Isles visit Man each year, enjoying the island's fine cliff scenery.*

The Manx nation was founded by Prince Orry in the tenth century after a tradition of varied Celtic, Scottish Gaelic, Welsh, and even Viking rulers. In 979, Prince Orry established the Manx Constitution, dividing the Isle of Man into six "Ship-shires" or "Sheadings." He also organized the law assembly, or "House of Keys" to which each "Sheading" elected four representatives. After the visit of St. Patrick on his way to Ireland in 444, Christianity played a large part in the development of the island. King Orry combined the authority of the Church and the high court or Tynwald Court which had the final authority in matters of justice. The court consisted of two appointed men who were called "Deemsters." One duty of the Deemsters which persists today is to recite to the public on Tynwald Day all new laws passed in that year; therefore, no one could claim ignorance of the law.

In 1429 the Stanley family was given the title of Lords of the Island by King Henry IV; they reigned until 1763 when the Athol family gained possession. In 1765 all material rights were sold to the British Crown.

The material wealth of the island was developed by the Monks of the Cistercian Order, an austere and industrious offshoot of the Benedictine Order. They recorded the earliest transcript of Manx history in the document *Chronicon Manniae*. Their Rushen Abbey was built by the Abbot of Furness, grandson of King Orry, and was known worldwide for its fine wool. Gradually the Order obtained control of all the best agricultural land, as well as the mining and fishing industries. The Abbey prospered until it was dissolved in 1541 by King Henry VIII.

The mining industry contributed not only lead, silver, zinc, and copper, but also one of the more famous tourist attractions of the island—the "Laxey Wheel" or the "Lady Isabella," which is the largest water-powered wheel in the world. It was designed by Robert Casement and built in 1854. There has been no mining on the island since 1900.

It is important to note that although the British Crown bought the material possessions, the island still governs itself as it did 1,000 years ago under King Orry, primarily with the three governing authorities: the King or Lord, the Governor and Council, and the House of Keys.

Shari Style

*Commemorating the millenium anniversary of the history and Parliament of the Isle of Man, many items have been produced. The silver "Manx Scenic Salver" pictured here is one of the finest.*

*Showing two famous Manx scenes—that of Tynwald Hill and The Laxey Wheel. These are surmounted by the Millenium Symbol commemorating 1,000 years of unbroken Parliamentary Government.*

*Tynwald Hill is the ancient three-tiered mound, said to have been created by earth brought from the seventeen parishes of the Island, and it is here the Manx Government meets each year in order that new laws may be promulgated. This ceremony has been maintained, it is believed, since as early as 1237.*

*The Laxey Wheel—"The Lady Isabella"—is the largest water-powered wheel in the world and was designed by the Manxman, Robert Casement, and built by the Island's craftsmen in 1854. This is a remarkable achievement of engineering for, when in use, the wheel pumped water from a depth of 1,000 feet at the rate of 250 gallons per minute. Now fully restored, but no longer in use, it is familiar to thousands of visitors from all over the world.*

Photograph Opposite
Laxey Wheel
Isle of Man

Overleaf Photograph
Port Erin, Isle of Man

# August Scene

Fern-carpeted, the woodland floor
Slants to the rocky river's shore,
Where beavers building twiggy domes
Construct their little brush-brown homes.

Beyond, reflected with the sky,
Rise sleepy hilltops, mountain-high,
And at the river's splashy brink
Two thirsty deer have come to drink.

Past woods and stream a meadow spreads
All bright with breezy daisy heads,
While edging it, an old church stands,
In proudly tended, farm-clad lands.

There seems no end to summer's hold,
But soon the green must turn to gold
As autumn beckons to the flowers
And stems the warmth of sun-kissed hours.

Louise Weibert Sutton

# Lakeside Reflections

From the magic of misty mountains
To the sunlight through dappled trees,
Time spent at the lake restores the soul
With nature's comforting ease.

From the distant blue of far-off hills
To the brightly shining sun,
The day is full of beauty
From dawn till evening's done.

There's the gentle touch of the morning breeze
And the warmth of sun-kissed earth,
The bracing cold of an early swim
And the birds' bright song of mirth.

There's the dazzling white of the sparkling lake
And the cool, soft shade of leaves
Where trees arch to the skyline,
And the shadow a pattern weaves.

The pure white whisps of morning mist
Float away across the bay,
And the sun streaks gold on a field of green
On this shining, shimmering day.

Some fleeting moments are impressed
Forever on our heart,
The bright scarlet streak of a cardinal,
The woodpecker's frenzied dart,

Water lapping on the shoreline,
The forget-me-nots wedgewood blue,
The clear white and yellow of daisies,
A cobweb, shining and new,

The roughness of the gnarled old oak,
The birch trees smooth gray bark,
The soft green springiness of moss
From light to velvet dark.

These are the things we dream of
When summer days are done,
Such memories stay within our hearts
In the glow of the setting sun.

Joan MacDonald

# PENNY CANDY

Once upon a time we kids went shopping,
Shopping with a penny, nothing more;
Walked along the streets, our hearts a-singing,
Right into the corner candy store.

There we saw the biggest candy counter—
What a sight for little eyes to see!
Sugar plums, and candy hearts, and suckers,
Chocolate men, as tempting as could be!

Lemon sticks, and lic'rice whips, and gumdrops,
Chocolates of every kind and size,
Caramels, and candy canes, and whistles,
Lying there before our hungry eyes!

But we had to do a bit of fig'ring;
A penny's worth just had to do for two!
One lic'rice whip or candy cane wouldn't answer,
As any hungry little kid plainly knew.

We hoped some day each one would have a penny,
A penny all his own with which to buy
Anything that cost a whole big penny,
Like a chocolate man or candy ice cream pie.

Alas, those days we only had a penny,
So peppermints were what we usu'lly got.
Six of them we bought for our one penny.
Three for each! That surely was a lot!

But nowadays when our kids go candy shopping,
A penny? Goodness no, they need a dime!
But I just bet their candy bar's no sweeter
Than our peppermints of once upon a time.

Clara M. Bode

# Memories of Home

Summer twilight brings back memories
Of a home beside the lane
Where the blossoms on the plum tree
Dripped perfume in the rain,

And the plaintive notes at sunset
As birdlings settled down
In the garden's flowering fragrance
And the glow of twilight's crown.

Very well do I remember
The creaking wooden gate,
And the fun of swinging on it
As for Father I would wait.

To his shoulder I was lifted
And had the tallest ride
As we galloped to the kitchen
And a table well-supplied.

Those balmy summer evenings
When the golden sun had set,
We heard robins in the clearing
And the whippoorwill duet.

There was stirring in the garden
As crickets sang their song,
And the silvery moon in rising
Splendored the whole night long.

I shall not forget the vision
Of a cottage neat and plain
Nestling near a peaceful hill
And a winding country lane.

And when daylight slowly faded
Shining lamplight took its place
And the soft warmth of the kitchen
Brought a glow to Mother's face.

Long years since then I've wandered
But memory serves me still,
For life flowed on serenely
As a benediction will.

Wild roses trailed the roadside
Wafting a fragrant mist
Through the doorway of a cottage,
A home by heaven kissed.

Katheryn Chouinard

I like to remember days gone by,
Old-fashioned kind of days,
When living was slow and easy
And simple were life's ways.

I like to travel the old roads
Past meadows, and forests, and farms,
Where new mown hay lies drying,
And the sun shines bright and warm.

I like to climb a mountain,
Stop by a rushing rill;
Watching the fish in the quiet pools
Is still a childlike thrill.

I like to chat with old folks
Who know of life this way,
Who help me recall the joys that were
In a time called yesterday.

Hildreth L. Patch

## Nostalgia

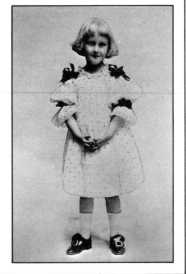

## A Great American Dessert

Can you think of an eighty-two-year-old American tradition that comes in sixteen flavors—and quivers? It's Jell-O,® of course, that versatile flavored gelatin product that has shimmered and sparkled on dining tables since 1895. Jell-O might easily challenge apple pie and ice cream in a contest to choose America's favorite dessert. Although it has found its way into sophisticated molds and literally hundreds of salad combinations, Jell-O is still synonymous with dessert for many adults.

The popularity of Jell-O is understandable. It's easy to prepare, pretty to look at, delicious to eat, and nutritionally sound. Jell-O has been the star of the spring luncheon, the colorful centerpiece at the bridal shower, and the light and luscious finale to even the fanciest holiday feast.

Versatile? Jell-O can be whipped, cubed, flaked, mounded, layered, molded. Almost every fruit and vegetable appears in Jell-O, one way or another; and its flavors can be enhanced with the addition of cream cheese, cottage cheese, sour cream, cola or ginger ale, marshmallows, or even candy "red hots." My mother often said that if you had a box of Jell-O in your pantry and a little imagination in your head, you'd always have dessert on hand.

Because Jell-O is so easy to digest and is a good source of liquid, parents have often dispensed a dish of Jell-O along with prescribed medicines to cure those sore throats and fevers of childhood. Through the years, many American youngsters have recuperated from a tonsillectomy with the help of hugs, sympathy, and a bowl of Jell-O. The cool, colorful gelatin treat has perked up many a flagging appetite.

How did Jell-O begin? It goes all the way back to 1845 and Peter Cooper, inventor of the famous locomotive "Tom Thumb." Cooper obtained the first patent for a gelatin dessert; and although he knew he had a saleable idea, he never pursued it. In 1895 Pearl B. Wait, a manufacturer of cough syrup and patent medicines in LeRoy, New York, adapted Cooper's gelatin dessert and started production in 1897. Wait's wife coined the name "Jell-O" for her husband's product.

Sales were poor, however, and Wait didn't have the expertise to extensively develop and market the product; so he sold it for $450 to his neighbor Orator F. Woodward. By the turn of the century, the public was clamoring for more of the powdered product, and sales skyrocketed. In 1902 Woodward placed his first ad in the *Ladies Home Journal* and in 1904 the "Jell-O Girl" made her debut. The original model was Elizabeth King, daughter of Franklin King, an artist for the company's advertising agency. In 1908 the Jell-O Girl became a part of the package design.

In the 1930s Jell-O became associated with America's beloved comedian Jack Benny. Benny's radio program, featuring Mary Livingston, announcer Don Wilson, and Kenny Baker with the Jell-O Orchestra, was heard by millions of Americans every Sunday night on the NBC Red Network. Benny worked with other sponsors during his long and successful radio career, but it was with Jell-O that he was most strongly identified. At the end of each show, when the Jell-O jingle was played, America sang along; and homemakers by the thousands sent to the General Foods Corporation for copies of *Jack and Mary's Jell-O Recipe Book*, complete with cartoon drawings of the two famous personalities.

In 1933, the homemaker could send a mere quarter to General Foods and receive either the six individual molds or one large mold in which to fashion a Strawberry Surprise. Today, collectors of advertising memorabilia are overjoyed to discover a set of the small aluminum Jell-O molds when they stalk flea markets or estate sales.

From an original offering of "six delicious flavors," Jell-O grew to a repertoire of sixteen flavors. Through the years, production and packaging techniques were modernized. At first, packages were filled by hand; but in 1914, the seamless sealed waxed paper bag was invented and it became possible to package the gelatin automatically.

For eighty-five years, Jell-O has remained popular; until today it is a staple in most kitchen cupboards. So move over apple pie and ice cream, and make room for Jell-O. It will shimmer for many years to come as an all-purpose, all-occasion, all-American treat.

Bea Bourgeois

I Remember When . . ..
We Changed Kitchens
Each Summer

Adeline Roseberg

In the days when farm cooking was done on wood stoves, many farm families had a "summer kitchen." This separate little building was used for cooking and eating during the hot summer season as well as for washing clothes, canning berries and vegetables, and making pickles and jelly. The use of a summer kitchen kept "the big house" cooler for sleeping, cleaner for entertaining company and freer from flies.

The summer kitchen was just one big room, furnished with only the bare necessities—the wood stove; a cupboard in one corner to hold dishes, pots and pans; and some nails on the wall near the stove to hang the two dishpans and a couple of frying pans.

A commode near the door held the pail of water with its dipper, the wash basin and a dish of soap. The room was furnished with a long table with benches for the children, chairs for Papa and Mamma and a high chair for the baby. (There was always a baby!)

"Moving into the summer kitchen" was an exciting day! On that day, we all helped to clean the kitchen thoroughly—sweeping the walls, washing the windows and furniture, and scrubbing the board floor one square at a time with scrub brush and laundry soap until it was white. The finishing touches were pure delight—putting a bright strip of woven rug on the floor, a gay new flowered or checkered oilcloth on the table, a bouquet of flowers in a fruit jar in the middle of the table and fresh window curtains, made from flour sacks trimmed with rickrack.

The next step was to help carry the necessities from the house—a minimum of dishes, silverware, towels and various odds and ends.

The first meal of the season in the summer kitchen was extra festive. Eating that day was like being away from home on a camping trip.

I remember lots of good eating in that summer kitchen . . . pancakes in the morning with blueberry sauce, Mamma's famous rye bread with our meals . . . and the radishes, green onions, and leaf lettuce from the garden. And later, there were big kettles of creamed peas and new potatoes, string beans and bacon, corn-on-the-cob and chicken soup.

But, also I remember what a problem the flies were! With all the good cooking aromas coming from that wood stove, flies settled thick on the old screen door, just waiting to get in. Furthermore, the door was often open—with so many of us children running in and out.

At the end of summer when the days became a bit chilly and the heat from a kitchen fire felt welcome once again, we moved back into the big house. This, too, was exciting, like coming home from a trip!

Today, gas and electric ranges predominate in farm homes, and the old summer kitchens are long gone. But, for some of us, they are still part of happy childhood memories.

# Picnic Classics

The old-fashioned family picnic is a sentimental repast that every American knows by heart from the deviled eggs to the watermelon. This familial feast has sparked some great picnic classics—foods that typify the wholesome charm of the American kitchen. While the cooking is traditional, it need not be routine or unimaginative. The homespun picnic won its acclaim on specialties that were the equal of any epicurean dish.

Today, alas, the majority of old-fashioned picnics are straight from the little old supermarket. Despite what the label proclaims, "Grannie's Old-Time Products" can't compete with your own freshly made salads and meats. Homespun picnics must be homespun.

The time and effort involved in preparing a hamperful of treats are well repaid by the salute you'll receive from your troops, for a family still travels on its stomach. The better the food, the happier the outing.

Give this picnic the affectionate preparation it deserves. It's just as important as any other picnic—maybe more so.

Nancy Fair McIntyre

### WATERMELON BASKET

½ watermelon
1 cantaloupe
1 qt. strawberries
1 qt. blueberries
1 qt. cherries
3 limes

Make large watermelon balls from the watermelon, discarding seeds. Leave only the shell. Make smaller balls from the cantaloupe. With a sharp knife trim the edge of the watermelon shell. Cut 1-inch triangles all the way around, making a decorative sawtooth edge. Insert the knife slantwise, make an incision 1-inch deep. Next to it make another incision slanted in the opposite direction to finish the triangle point. Repeat all around, cutting one triangle out and leaving one standing up.

Fill the shell with melon balls, adding strawberries, blueberries and cherries. Pile the fruit high in the shell. Decorate with 3 quartered limes and a few mint leaves. Chill before serving.

### OVEN-FRIED CHICKEN

1 2- to 3-lb. chicken, cut up
1 stick butter
1½ c. flour
1 c. bread crumbs
1 t. salt
1 t. paprika
1 t. poultry seasoning
1 t. black pepper
1 c. canned milk

Wash chicken, drain. Season to taste with salt and pepper. Mix remaining dry ingredients. Dip chicken in milk; roll in flour and bread crumb mixture. Place in a large pan. Melt butter and spoon over chicken. Bake for 1 hour in a preheated 325° oven.

Mildred King

### LEMONADE REFRESHER

1 c. water
1 c. sugar
1 c. lemon juice
4 c. water

Combine sugar and water in a saucepan. Heat, stirring constantly, until sugar dissolves. Bring to a full rolling boil. Cool. Add lemon juice and water. Fill glasses. Add ice cubes.

PICNIC CLASSICS by Nancy McIntyre. From IT'S A PICNIC! by Nancy Fair McIntyre, Copyright © 1969 by Nancy McIntyre. First published in 1969 by The Viking Press Inc. Reprinted with permission of Viking Penguin Inc.

# The Sounds of Youth

Most of my early life was spent in small towns. You would take a walk and within a half hour you would be out of the town's limits. Then it was that you would hear sounds from night birds, the distant whistle of locomotives, perhaps a church bell or whistle of the wind.

It was on the farm, however, that the most familiar sounds seemed to cluster. How many times during the summer I was fascinated by the distant clang of the cowbell! To this day it is magic to my ears. A few years ago I came across one of those bells and during my vacations I carry it with me, as a reminder of my youth.

My father, being a minister, I had the job as janitor of the church, and so rang the big bell, calling people to worship. In the country I loved the calls and songs of the birds, the meadowlark, the night hawks, the whippoorwill, wild pigeons, the bobolink, and many others.

I recall how amusing and pleasant, was the churr of the crickets, and how friendly they seemed. Another familiar sound was that of the frogs in the pools and small lakes near town. What a world of mystery and magic the youth of today miss who have never experienced farm life, and who have missed the brilliance of the stars on a clear night. I used to sit with my mother on the "front steps" and just listen!

Nature is full of sounds and music. And in daylight the call of various birds is enchanting. I would be lonely without their friendly songs, and their cheerful way of life, no matter where I might live.

George Matthew Adams

# It Is July

When the scarlet cardinal tells
   Her dream to the dragonfly,
And the lazy breeze makes a nest in the trees,
   And murmurs a lullaby,
     It is July.

When the tangled cobweb pulls
   The cornflower's cap awry,
And the lilies tall lean over the wall
   To bow to the butterfly,
     It is July.

When the heat like a mist veil floats,
   And poppies flame in the rye,
And the silver note in the streamlet's throat
   Has softened almost to a sigh,
     It is July.

When the hours are so still that time
   Forgets them, and lets them lie
Neath petals pink till the night stars wink
   At the sunset in the sky,
     It is July.

Susan Hartley Swett

# Poppies

Poppies on a hillside,
   Yellow, orange, and gold!
Poppies in profusion,
   Yes, a thousandfold!

Dancing in the sunshine,
   Flirting with the trees,
Poppies nodding gaily
   In the summer breeze!

Alice Winquist Burmont

# The Great Stone Face

Nathaniel Hawthorne

The Great Stone Face was a work of nature in her mood of majestic playfulness, formed on the perpendicular side of a mountain by some immense rocks, which had been thrown together in such a position as, when viewed at a proper distance, precisely to resemble the features of the human countenance.

It was a happy lot for children to grow up to manhood or womanhood with the Great Stone Face before their eyes, for all the features were noble, and the expression was at once grand and sweet, as if it were the glow of a vast, warm heart that embraced all mankind in its affections, and had room for more.

A mother and her little boy sat at their cottage door, gazing at the Great Stone Face, and talking about it. The child's name was Ernest.

So his mother told him a story that her own mother had told her, when she herself was younger than little Ernest; a story, not of things that were past, but of what was yet to come; a story, nevertheless, so very old that even the Indians, who formerly inhabited this valley, had heard it from their forefathers, to whom, as they affirmed, it had been murmured by the mountain streams, and whispered by the wind among the treetops. The purport was that at some future day a child should be born hereabouts who was destined to become the greatest and noblest personage of his time, and whose countenance, in manhood, should bear an exact resemblance to the Great Stone Face.

And Ernest never forgot the story that his mother told him. It was always in his mind, whenever he looked upon the Great Stone Face. He spent his childhood in the log cottage where he was born, and was dutiful to his mother, and helpful to her in many things, assisting her much with his little hands, and more with his loving heart. In this manner, from a happy yet often pensive child, he grew up to be a mild, quiet, unobtrusive boy, and sun-browned with labor in the fields, but with more intelligence brightening his aspect than is seen in many lads who have been taught at famous schools.

About this time there went a rumor throughout the valley that the great man, foretold from ages long ago, who was to bear a resemblance to the Great Stone Face, had appeared at last. It seems that, many years before, a young man had migrated from the valley and settled at a distant seaport where, after getting together a little money, he had set up as a shopkeeper. His name—but I never could learn whether it was a real one, or a nickname that had grown out of his habits and success in life—was Gathergold. Being shrewd and active, he became an exceedingly rich merchant, and owner of a whole fleet of ships. It might be said of him, as of Midas in the fable, that whatever he touched with his finger immediately glistened, and grew yellow, and was changed at once into piles of coins.

And, when Mr. Gathergold had become so very rich, he bethought himself of his native valley, and resolved to go back thither and end his days where he was born.

"Here he comes!" cried a group of people who were assembled to witness the arrival. "Here comes the great Mr. Gathergold!"

A carriage, drawn by four horses, dashed round the turn of the road. Within it, thrust partly out of the window, appeared the old man, with skin as yellow as if his own Midas-hand had transmuted it. He had a low forehead, small sharp eyes, puckered about with innumerable wrinkles, and very thin lips, which he made still thinner by pressing them forcibly together.

"The very image of the Great Stone Face!" shouted the people. "Sure enough, the old prophecy is true; and here we have the great man, come at last!"

And, what greatly perplexed Ernest, they seemed actually to believe that here was the likeness which they spoke of. By the roadside there chanced to be an old beggar woman and two little children, who, as the carriage rolled onward, held out their hands and lifted up their voices, beseeching charity. A yellow claw poked itself out of the coach window, and dropped some copper coins upon the ground; so that, though the great man's name seemed to have been Gathergold, he might just as suitably have been nicknamed Scattercopper. Still, with an earnest shout, and evidently with as much good faith as ever, the people shouted, "He is the very image of the Great Stone Face!"

But Ernest turned sadly from the wrinkled shrewdness of that sordid visage, and gazed up the valley where, amid a gathering mist, gilded by the last sunbeams, he could still distinguish those glorious

features which had impressed themselves into his soul. Their aspect cheered him. What did the benign lips seem to say?

"He will come? Fear not, Ernest; the man will come!"

More years sped swiftly and tranquilly away. Ernest still dwelt in his native valley, and was now a man of middle age. By imperceptible degrees, he had become known among the people. Now, as heretofore, he labored for his bread, and was the same simple-hearted man that he had always been. But he had thought and felt so much, he had given so many of the best hours of his life to unworldly hopes for some great good to mankind, that it seemed as though he had been talking with angels, and had imbibed a portion of their wisdom unawares. It was visible in the calm and well-considered beneficence of his daily life. Not a day passed by, that the world was not the better because this man, humble as he was, had lived.

Almost involuntarily, too, he had become a lecturer. The pure and high simplicity of his thought, which, as one of its manifestations, took shape in the good deeds that dropped silently from his hand, flowed also forth in speech. He uttered truths that wrought upon and moulded the lives of those who heard him. His auditors never suspected that Ernest, their own neighbor and familiar friend, was more than an ordinary man; least of all did Ernest himself suspect it.

But now, again, there were reports and many paragraphs in the newspapers affirming that the likeness of the Great Stone Face had appeared upon the broad shoulders of a certain eminent statesman. He, like Mr. Gathergold was a native of the valley, but had left it in his early days, and had taken up the trades of law and politics.

"Here he is, now!" cried those who stood near Ernest. "There! There! Look at Old Stony Phiz and then at the Old Man of the Mountain, and see if they are not as like as two twin brothers!"

In the midst of all this gallant array came an open coach, drawn by four white horses; and in the coach, with his massive head uncovered, sat the illustrious statesman, Old Stony Phiz himself.

Now it must be owned that, at his first glimpse of the countenance which was bowing and smiling from the coach, Ernest did fancy that there was a resemblance between it and the old familiar face upon the mountainside. The brow, with its massive depth and loftiness, and all the other features, indeed, were boldly and strongly hewn. But the sublimity and stateliness, the grand expression of a divine sympathy, that illuminated the mountain visage, might here be sought in vain. Something had been originally left out, or had departed. And therefore the marvelously gifted statesman had a weary gloom in the deep caverns of his eyes, as a man of mighty faculties and little aims, whose life,

with all its high performances, was vague and empty, because no high purpose had endowed it with reality.

Ernest turned away, melancholy, and almost despondent: for this was the saddest of his disappointments, to behold a man who might have fulfilled the prophecy, and had not willed to do so.

The years hurried onward, and now they began to bring white hairs, and scatter them over the head of Ernest; they made reverend wrinkles across his forehead, and furrows in his cheeks. He was an aged man. But not in vain had he grown old: more than the white hairs on his head were the sage thoughts in his mind. His wrinkles and furrows were inscriptions that Time had engraved, and in which were written legends of wisdom that had been tested by the tenor of a life.

And Ernest had ceased to be obscure. Unsought for, undesired, had come the fame which so many seek, and made him known in the great world, beyond the limits of the valley in which he had dwelt so quietly. College professors, and even the active men of cities, came from far to see and converse with Ernest; for the report had gone abroad that this simple husbandman had ideals unlike those of other men, not gained from books, but of a higher tone—a tranquil and familiar majesty, as if he had been talking with the angels as his daily friends.

While Ernest had been growing up and growing old, a bountiful Providence had granted a new poet to this earth. He, likewise, was a native of the valley, but had spent the greater part of his life at a distance from that romantic region, pouring out his sweet music amid the bustle and din of cities. Often, however, did the mountains which had been familiar to him in his childhood lift their snowy peaks into the clear atmosphere of his poetry. This man of genius had wonderful endowments. Thus the world assumed another and a better aspect from the hour that the poet blessed it with his happy eyes.

The songs of this poet found their way to Ernest. He read them after his customary toil, seated on the bench before his cottage door, where for such a length of time he had filled his repose with thought, by gazing at the Great Stone Face. And now as he read stanzas that caused the soul to thrill within him, he lifted his eyes to the vast countenance beaming on him so benignantly.

"O majestic friend," he murmured, addressing the Great Stone Face, "is not this man worthy to resemble thee?" The face seemed to smile, but answered not a word.

Now this poet, though he dwelt so far away, had not only heard of Ernest, but had meditated much upon his character, until he deemed nothing so desirable as to meet this man, whose untaught wisdom walked hand in hand with the noble simplicity of his life. One summer morning, therefore, he took passage by railroad, and alighted from the cars at no great distance from Ernest's cottage.

Approaching the door, he therefore found the good old man, holding a volume in his hand, which alternately he read, and then, with a finger between the leaves, looked lovingly at the Great Stone Face.

"Good evening," said the poet. "Can you give a traveler a night's lodging?"

"Willingly," answered Ernest, smiling.

The poet sat down on the bench beside him, and he and Ernest talked together. Often had the poet held intercourse with the wittiest and the wisest, but never before with a man like Ernest, whose thoughts and feelings gushed up with such a natural freedom, and who made great truths so familiar by his simple utterance of them. Angels, as had been so often said, seemed to have wrought with him at his labor in the fields; angels seemed to have sat with him by the fireside; and, dwelling with angels as friends, he had imbibed the sublimity of their ideas, and imbued it with the sweet and lowly charm of household words. So thought the poet.

And Ernest, on the other hand, was moved and agitated by the living images which the poet flung out of his mind. The sympathies of these two men instructed them with a profounder sense than either could have attained alone. Their minds accorded into one strain, and made delightful music which neither of them could have claimed as all his own, nor distinguished his own share from the other's.

As Ernest listened to the poet, he imagined that the Great Stone Face was bending forward to listen too. He gazed earnestly into the poet's glowing eyes.

"Who are you, my strangely gifted guest?" he said. The poet laid his finger on the volume that Ernest had been reading.

"You have read these poems," said he. "You know me, then—for I wrote them."

Again, and still more earnestly than before, Ernest examined the poet's features; then turned toward the Great Stone Face; then back, with an uncertain aspect, to his guest. But his countenance fell; he shook his head, and sighed.

"Wherefore are you sad?" inquired the poet.

"Because," replied Ernest, "all through life I have awaited the fulfillment of a prophecy; and when I read these poems, I hoped that it might be fulfilled in you."

"You hoped," answered the poet, faintly smiling, "to find in me the likeness of the Great Stone Face. And you are disappointed, as formerly with Mr. Gathergold and Old Stony Phiz. Yes, Ernest, it is my doom. You must add my name to theirs, and record another failure of your hopes. For—in shame and sadness do I speak it, Ernest—I am not worthy to be typified by yonder benign and majestic image."

"And why?" asked Ernest. He pointed to the volume. "Are not these thoughts divine?"

"They have a strain of the Divinity," replied the poet. "You can hear in them the far-off echo of a heavenly song. But my life, dear Ernest, has not corresponded with my thought. I have had grand dreams, but they have been only dreams, because I have lived—and that, too, by my own choice—among poor and mean realities. Sometimes even—shall I dare to say it?—I lack faith in the grandeur, the beauty, and the goodness which my own works are said to have made more evident in nature and in human life. Why, then, pure seeker of the good and true, shouldst thou hope to find in me yonder image of the divine?"

The poet spoke sadly, and his eyes were dim with tears. So, likewise, were those of Ernest.

At the hour of sunset, as had long been his frequent custom, Ernest was to discourse at an assemblage of the neighboring inhabitants in the open air. He and the poet, arm in arm, still talking together as they went along, proceeded to the spot.

At a small elevation there appeared a niche. Into this natural pulpit Ernest ascended, and threw a look of familiar kindness around upon his audience. In another direction was seen the Great Stone Face, with the same cheer, combined with the same solemnity, in its benignant aspect.

Ernest began to speak, giving to the people of what was in his heart and mind. His words had power, because they accorded with his thoughts; and his thoughts had reality and depth, because they harmonized with the life which he had always lived. It was not mere breath that he uttered; they were the words of life, because a life of good deeds and holy love was melted into them.

At that moment, in sympathy with a thought which he was about to utter, the face of Ernest assumed a grandeur of expression, so imbued with benevolence, that the poet, by an irresistible impulse, threw his arms aloft and shouted, "Behold! Behold! Ernest is himself the likeness of the Great Stone Face?"

Then all the people looked, and saw that what the deep-sighted poet said was true! The prophecy was fulfilled.

But Ernest, having finished what he had to say, took the poet's arm, and walked slowly homeward, still hoping that some wiser and better man than himself would by and by appear, bearing a resemblance to the Great Stone Face.

# The Simple Things

Oh let us keep the simple things,
The charms an early morning brings,
The meadow grass all fresh with dew
Before the sun comes stealing through,
Majestic mountains reaching high
That seem to kiss the blue of sky.

Oh let us love the things so small
That sometimes matter not at all,
One tiny bird upon her nest,
When quiet minds would pause in rest,
The babbling brook, a shaded place,
Or just one smile upon a face.

Oh let us love the gentle rain,
The growing wheat upon the plain,
A wildflower bringing beauty rare,
The scent of lilacs on the air,
The peaceful moments with a friend
Just as the rush of day would end.

A tiny child with trusting eyes,
A rainbow after stormy skies,
Bright colors of an autumn day,
A smile of God where sunbeams play,
The wondrous gladness loving brings
Oh, let us keep the simple things.

Garnett Ann Schultz

# August

I love the brooks and whispering streams
   That flow so gently on;
I love the lakes where sunshine gleams,
   The ponds reflecting song.

I love the open countryside,
   The hills and valleys too;
I love the meadows, flowered wide
   With asters brightly blue.

I love the fields of tassled corn,
   The land with golden grain;
I love the misty silent morn,
   The footstep of the rain.

I love the sound of birds on wing,
   The rustling of the leaves;
I love the words that branches sing,
   The soft and soothing breeze.

I love the mountains far away,
   The coolness of the night;
I love the stars in wide array,
   The moon so wise and bright.

Gertrude Rudberg

# Portrait of an American Hero

When it comes to the heroes America claims,
   There's a lot to be said for the simple names,
Referring especially to one John Wayne,
   For everyone knows and loves that name.

He was Iowa born—a real "country" lad,
   Brought up on the homespun advice of his dad.
"Good character, son, makes a man be his best.
   It's far more important than wealth or success."

Young John was six when they pulled up stakes
   And moved out west with the rattlesnakes.
The labor was constant, and danger was worse,
   But he learned how to shoot well and handle a horse.

John turned nine, and they moved to town.
   He and his friends used to hang around
And watch all the westerns being made—
   Dreaming of parts they'd love to have played.

Later, the "Duke" (as his name had become),
   Would romp with his friends "movie-making" for fun.
Little they knew that the heroes they'd play
   Would all be surpassed by the Duke someday.

Wayne's success took its own sweet time;
   Every step was an uphill climb.
For forty-some years he struggled away
   To achieve the renown he has today.

*The Cowboys, Chisum, How the West Was Won;*
   At last count the number was one-fifty-some.
*Hatari, The Alamo*—all of the rest,
   But most, by far, say, *True Grit* was his best.

Portraying all types from A to Z:
   Cowboys and coal miners, men of the sea,
Duke will admit that his best-played roles
   Are the ones which reflect his heart and his soul.

As common as sun, and wind, and rain,
   "Big Duke" is in the American grain.
Solid as an oak tree with deep-spreading roots,
   America stands proud as John Wayne she salutes.

Linda C. Robinson

# Church
## in the Valley

Deep in a valley, lush and green,
A wooden church stands near a pine;
Its glistening steeple may be seen
With a golden cross in bright sunshine.

And from the hilltop near our home,
Where in the summer daisies grow,
I like to wander there alone
To watch the scenery below.

The branches seem to wave to me,
As though inviting me to come
To church beside the lone pine tree
So friendly in the shining sun.

Elsie Natalie Brady

# The Little White House

*Grace Bush*

*There's a little white house by the shining sea,*
*And the hours spent there are dear to me;*
*For first you climb up a little hill*
*And there it is sitting, so sweet and still.*
*Under the windows daisies white*
*Spread their snowy blooms in the bright sunlight,*
*Petunias, nasturtiums and pansies grow*
*And cluster about it, row on row!*

And in the cool breeze, hollyhocks
Curtsy like ladies in gay new frocks.
Then up the step to a little red door,
Nicer than any you've seen before,
That seems to say, as it opens wide,
"Welcome, dear guest! Please step inside!

Here is a little haven to rest,
For the sun is sinking in the west,
I will give you peace for your heart to hold,
And beauty to warm you when you're cold,
I'll care for you all through the night
And guard you safe, till the morning light
Wakes you to throw your window wide!
Welcome, dear guest! Please step inside!"

There are braided mats on the shining floor,
Woven by fingers in days of yore;
And willow cups and plates of blue
That whisper, "We'd like to have tea with you!"
And such an intriguing shelf of books,

That coax you to turn a page and look;
And two of the quaintest rocking chairs,
With cushions and ruffles to give them airs,
That seem to hold out their arms and smile
"Won't you stay and gossip awhile?"

Dear little house, it grieves my heart
To think that you and I must part,
That you must stay here by the shining sea
And it's back to the busy world for me!
So radiant, so sweet were the sunny hours
That I spent with you among the flowers,
And I'll hold you close in my memory
Dear little house by the shining sea!

Ideals' Pages
from the Past

School

ideals

On the following six pages
we are presenting a selection
from School Ideals 1949.

# SCHOOL DAYS

Glad vacation days are gone—
My, how swiftly they have flown,
And once again we hear
  The school bells ring;
Calling to our girls and boys;
Come, forsake vacation joys,
To greet once more the tasks
  That school days bring.

And in answer to the call,
We see the children great and small,
Come trudging down the country
  Road, or street;
With their eyes so clear and bright,
And their hearts carefree and light;
As they bravely go once more
  Their tasks to meet.

On the playground o'er the way,
We hear the children at their play,
And school rooms long so still
  Resound once more,
With their happy shouts of cheer
As they greet their teacher dear—
As you and I once did
  In days of yore.

Glad vacation days are o'er
And it is study time once more;
Children, see each golden hour
  You wisely spend.
Do each task assigned to you,
Be to self and teachers true,
And success will surely
  Greet you in the end.

*Our sincere thanks to
the unknown author.*

# First Days

Helen Welshimer

Little red schools on a country road,
 And those on a city street,
Alike are echoing once again
 To the marching of eager feet.
Faces with freckles and faces with smiles,
 Sometimes a tear in an eye,
Now and again there's a new little girl,
 Or a little boy starting to cry.

Oh, the road winds far when it starts
 to school,
 And it wanders through half the town,
When a small boy chokes on a hidden
 lump
 That wants to go up, not down.
His toys are scattered about the house;
 Yesterday he could play,
But he washed his face and he went to
 school
 When the loud bell rang today.

He's finding a world that he didn't
 know,
 He'll laugh at each glad surprise,
After the lump goes down a bit
 And the tears have left his eyes.
The waiting toys are as safe as safe.
 It's part of an old, old rule:
Nobody likes to touch his toys
 When the last little boy's in school.

*Our sincere thanks to the author whose
address we were unable to locate.*

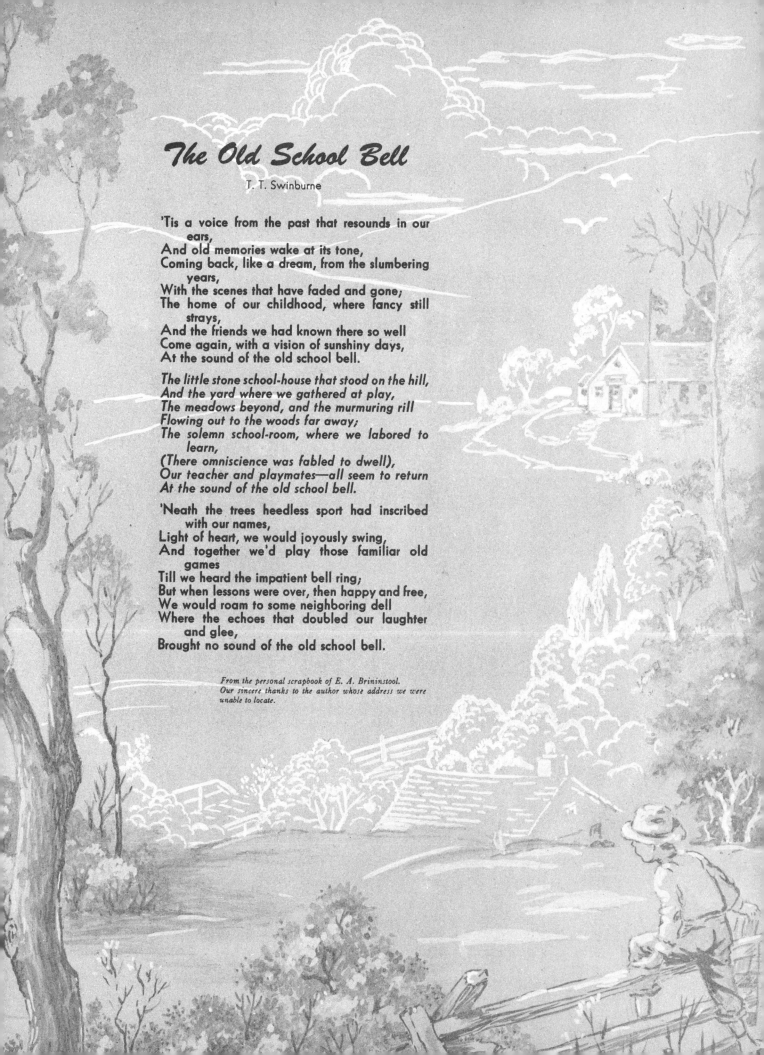

# The Old School Bell

### T. T. Swinburne

'Tis a voice from the past that resounds in our
    ears,
And old memories wake at its tone,
Coming back, like a dream, from the slumbering
    years,
With the scenes that have faded and gone;
The home of our childhood, where fancy still
    strays,
And the friends we had known there so well
Come again, with a vision of sunshiny days,
At the sound of the old school bell.

The little stone school-house that stood on the hill,
And the yard where we gathered at play,
The meadows beyond, and the murmuring rill
Flowing out to the woods far away;
The solemn school-room, where we labored to
    learn,
(There omniscience was fabled to dwell),
Our teacher and playmates—all seem to return
At the sound of the old school bell.

'Neath the trees heedless sport had inscribed
    with our names,
Light of heart, we would joyously swing,
And together we'd play those familiar old
    games
Till we heard the impatient bell ring;
But when lessons were over, then happy and free,
We would roam to some neighboring dell
Where the echoes that doubled our laughter
    and glee,
Brought no sound of the old school bell.

*From the personal scrapbook of E. A. Brininstool.
Our sincere thanks to the author whose address we were
unable to locate.*

Today is yesterday's pupil.

*B. Franklin*

The things that hurt, instruct.

*B. Franklin*

Justice is as strictly due between neighbor nations
as between neighbor citizens. A highwayman is as
much a robber when he plunders in a gang as when
single; and a nation that makes an unjust war is
only a great gang.

*B. Franklin*

Business not well managed ruins one faster than
no business.

*B. Franklin*

There are two ways of being happy. We must
either diminish our wants or augment our means—
either may do—the result is the same and it is for
each man to decide for himself as to that which
happens to be easier.

*B. Franklin*

They that can give up essential liberty to obtain
a little temporary safety deserve neither liberty
nor safety.

*B. Franklin*

Want of care does us more damage than want of
knowledge.

*B. Franklin*

Color Art and Photo Credits:
(in order of appearance)
Front cover: Chocorua, New Hampshire, Fred Sieb; Inside front cover: A QUIET PLACE, Frank Massa; color pages: A road along the Mississippi River, Fountain City, Wisconsin, Ken Dequaine; Delphiniums, Fred Sieb; Harry S. Truman home, Independence, Missouri, Freelance Photographers Guild; MOTHER AND CHILD, Four by Five, Inc.; Edison phonograph, Gerald Koser, Edison phonograph used, courtesy of Dan Luedtke; Parade, Montclair, New Jersey, A. Devaney, Inc.; Fireworks, A. Devaney, Inc.; Children on bridge, H. Armstrong Roberts; Butterfly on rose, Robert Cushman Hayes; Grand Canyon National Park, Arizona, Josef Muench; Laxey Wheel, Isle of Man, Colour Library International Limited; Port Erin showing Bradda Head, Isle of Man, Colour Library International Limited; Clair Engle Lake, California, Josef Muench; Harrisville, New Hampshire, Fred Dole; CANDY STORE by John Slobodnik; A GREAT AMERICAN DESSERT, Gerald Koser, items featured in photograph, courtesy of Roger C. Christensen; An old-fashioned picnic, Ralph Luedtke; Red poppies, Fred Sieb; OLD MAN OF THE MOUNTAINS, Franconia Notch, New Hampshire, Fred Sieb; Rolling farmland, La Crosse, Wisconsin, Ken Dequaine; Field of daisies, Fred Sieb; BACK TO SCHOOL, George Hinke; THE LIBERTY BELL'S FIRST NOTE, J. L. G. Farris; Inside back cover: PEACEFUL COUNTRY SIDE, Frank Massa; Back cover: Fred Sieb.

ACKNOWLEDGMENTS

THE SOUNDS OF YOUTH by George Matthew Adams. Reprinted by permission of Washington Star Syndicate, Inc. THESE PRICELESS THINGS by Ben Burroughs. SKETCHES by Ben Burroughs. Copyright 1965. General Features Corp. SWEET MUSIC by R. J. McGinnis. From THE GOOD OLD DAYS, edited and compiled by R. J. McGinnis, Copyright © 1960 by F and W Publishing Corporation. WE CHANGED KITCHENS EACH SUMMER by Adeline Roseberg. Reprinted from FARM WIFE NEWS, August 1976.

Coming in Autumn Ideals

A Grandparent's Day feature . . . the colorful world of Victorian Stained Glass, by Russell Zimmermann . . . the life work of Walter Lantz, famed creator of Woody Woodpecker . . . Ideals' Best-Loved Poet, Joy Belle Burgess . . . Pages from the Past, Autumn Ideals 1952 . . . along with poetry and prose reflecting the beautiful color of autumn.

# Introduce a special friend or relative to *ideals*

## CHOOSE A
# FREE GIFT

FOR EVERY NEW SUBSCRIPTION ORDERED!

You probably know a number of close friends who have enjoyed looking at your copies of Ideals over the past years. Close friends often share the same values . . . are touched by the same sentiments . . . are warmed by the same emotional expressions of love and joy—the very things contained in each and every issue of Ideals.

Now, for a limited time, we invite you to help us bring more wholesome beauty and simple joy into the lives of others. And, by simply helping a good friend or special relative discover the same honest pleasure and tranquil satisfaction that you enjoy in reading Ideals, we will thank you in a very special way.

Share your latest issue of Ideals with a friend. For each new 1-year or 2-year subscription that is ordered by one of your friends, relatives, or as a gift from you . . . you may choose one of the above books for yourself - free - as our special thank you.

We know your friends will enjoy Ideals as much as you do. It's a steadfast confirmation that in today's fast-paced world there is still room for feelings of faith, hope and love—the things in life that really matter. So don't wait . . . you and your friends may enter as many subscriptions as you wish. And for each new subscription you'll receive a FREE BOOK of your choice, and the satisfaction of brightening another's day through the pages of Ideals.

## LIMIT ONE FREE BOOK PER SUBSCRIPTION

## HURRY—OFFER EXPIRES SEPTEMBER 1, 1979

# IDEALS SUBSCRIPTION ORDERS

( ) Enter 1-Year (8 Issue) Subscription for $15.95 to:

( ) Enter 2-Year (16 Issue) Subscription for $27.95 to:

MY NAME _____

ADDRESS _____

CITY _____ STATE_____ ZIP _____

Outside USA - Add $2 Postage Per Subscription Year

---

### Send Me The Free Book Checked Below

□ Book A  □ Book B  □ Book C  □ Book D  □ Book E

NAME _____

ADDRESS _____

CITY _____ STATE_____ ZIP _____

( ) Payment Enclosed  ( ) Bill Top Name ( ) Bill Bottom Name

BG97

---

( ) Enter 1-Year (8 Issue) Subscription for $15.95 to:

( ) Enter 2-Year (16 Issue) Subscription for $27.95 to:

MY NAME _____

ADDRESS _____

CITY _____ STATE_____ ZIP _____

Outside USA - Add $2 Postage Per Subscription Year

---

### Send Me The Free Book Checked Below

□ Book A  □ Book B  □ Book C  □ Book D  □ Book E

NAME _____

ADDRESS _____

CITY _____ STATE_____ ZIP _____

( ) Payment Enclosed  ( ) Bill Top Name ( ) Bill Bottom Name

BG

---

FOLD HERE FIRST

BG97

FOLD SIDE FLAPS FIRST — THEN FOLD HERE

THANK YOU!

ZIP CODE

from

**ideals**
PUBLISHING CORPORATION
P.O. BOX 726
GREAT NECK, NEW YORK 11025

When properly sealed with the above gummed flap this envelope and its contents will travel safely through the mail.

FOLD HERE FIRST

---

( ) Enter 1-Year (8 Issue) Subscription for $15.95 to:

( ) Enter 2-Year (16 Issue) Subscription for $27.95 to:

MY NAME _____

ADDRESS _____

CITY _____ STATE_____ ZIP _____

Outside USA - Add $2 Postage Per Subscription Year

---

### Send Me The Free Book Checked Below

□ Book A  □ Book B  □ Book C  □ Book D  □ Book E

NAME _____

ADDRESS _____

CITY _____ STATE_____ ZIP _____

( ) Payment Enclosed  ( ) Bill Top Name ( ) Bill Bottom Name  BG97

---

( ) Enter 1-Year (8 Issue) Subscription for $15.95 to:

( ) Enter 2-Year (16 Issue) Subscription for $27.95 to:

MY NAME _____

ADDRESS _____

CITY _____ STATE_____ ZIP _____

Outside USA - Add $2 Postage Per Subscription Year

---

### Send Me The Free Book Checked Below

□ Book A  □ Book B  □ Book C  □ Book D  □ Book E

NAME _____

ADDRESS _____

CITY _____ STATE_____ ZIP _____

( ) Payment Enclosed  ( ) Bill Top Name ( ) Bill Bottom Name  BG